# The Official
# Hibernian
## Annual 2006

A Grange Publication

Written by David Forsyth

© 2005. Published by Grange Communications Ltd., Edinburgh, under licence from Hibernian Football Club. Printed in the EU.

ISBN 1 905426 00 3

£6.99

4

# Contents

# Introduction

Welcome to the Hibernian FC official 2006 Annual.

Profiles of the squad, interviews with the Manager Tony Mowbray, a review of last season month by month, quizzes, a look at the Club's great history and a snapshot of our achievements in Europe are all included in this edition.

We also feature the work of the Youth Academy, a profile of Mark Venus and a look at the goal-scoring exploits of Garry O'Connor.

We hope you enjoy reading the annual, and following the fortunes of your favourite football team!

# Manager Profile

When Tony Mowbray was unveiled as the new Hibernian Manager in May 2004 at a packed Press conference the sounds of cameras clicking and whirring were drowned by jaws hitting the floor!

During a search for Bobby Williamson's successor that had taken several weeks, media speculation had grown in intensity and almost every available manager in Scotland – and several who were already attached to other Clubs – was linked by the Press.

Several newspapers ran stories announcing with certainty that a named individual was THE candidate, and would be announced by the Club within hours. Not one prediction mentioned the man who would eventually fill the post.

But while Tony Mowbray was a surprise choice in the eyes of many, in the eyes of the Board he was the ideal choice.

The lengthy search had been meticulously undertaken, whittling down candidates and taking soundings, and measuring interested candidates against a set of criteria drawn up by the Board. Tony's application stood out, and once he was approached he immediately impressed Chief Executive Rod Petrie and non-executive director Steve Dunn, who were leading the hunt. Tony attended a meeting with the Board, and again impressed.

One key phrase he used at that meeting struck a chord: "My philosophy is all about fast-flowing, passing football with a cutting edge." When he used it again with the Media, it met with a rather more sceptical response, many pundits believing these were the words of an untested young coach.

Fast forward till the end of the season, and the same journalists – to their credit – have heaped praise on the thrilling young side put together by Tony Mowbray, Mark Venus and the rest of the coaching staff. Tony has been voted "Manager of the Year" by the Scottish Football Writers Association, and Derek Riordan named as Young Player of the Year.

Cont.

## Tony Mowbray Profile

8

## So does he think his work is done?

"Of course not. I said at the start that we were setting out on a journey, that there is no magic switch you can flick and suddenly start playing fantastic football. At times throughout last season we have shown our ability to play terrific passing football and to score great goals, but we are a long way short of the finished article. Our target must be to try and close the gap on the Old Firm – and that target must be shared by other Clubs in Scotland. It isn't good to see the Old Firm finishing the league 30 points clear of the rest, and we have to try to get closer.

"That's not to say we haven't improved. The players worked really hard last season and I think every player improved. That's one of the joys of working with young players – you are working with a blank canvas with lads who have a thirst and a hunger to learn and to improve."

Tony's coaching abilities were one of the key factors in his appointment. Five years spent as first-team coach at Ipswich, and in gaining his UEFA Pro license – the highest coaching qualifications – had prepared him for his role in management and those who had seen him develop his coaching skills spoke in the highest terms of his technical coaching abilities and knowledge.

But it was also the praise he received for his character and integrity, his qualities of leadership that persuaded the Board to appoint him. This, after all, was a man who played at three big Clubs and captained all of them. Again, these qualities have shone through during his spell at the helm.

" I think my own strengths are hopefully the person I am, a man of integrity I like to think. I can deal with individuals, I can communicate with them and hopefully gain their respect. I want to work with these young men and make them better footballers and better human beings, and they respond to that."

Cont.

9

## What of the future?

" I'd like to think we can continue to make progress, to improve this Club. The supporters are passionate about this Club and they want to see us winning, but winning in a certain way. So do I, and I will carry on doing my best to achieve it. Fast-flowing football, played at pace, lots of passing and scoring goals. And winning."

## Tony Mowbray factfile:

Tony Mowbray – Manager

Born: 22 November 1963 in Saltburn

Tony joined in May 2004 as Manager, following a five-year stint as player/first-team coach at Ipswich.

A highly respected player in his time, Tony turned out for Middlesbrough, Ipswich and – in Scotland – for Celtic. He captained all three Clubs.

A towering and dominant central defender, he was revered by fans at all three Clubs for his whole-hearted commitment and his will to win.

Tony Mowbray Profile

# Mark Venus Profile

Tony Mowbray is the first to acknowledge that management is a team game, and in tackling the challenge that faced him with Hibernian he turned to his former team-mate, defensive partner and close friend, Mark Venus.

Mark was Tony's first signing, unveiled in June 2004, and has since played a vital role supporting the Manager as he has developed the style of play which has attracted such praise.

Tony said: "I needed someone I could trust, someone who stimulates me and someone who shares my passion for the game and for studying the game. Mark has these qualities, and more. He works closely with the players, and they all respect him for his talent and for the way he treats them."

The move north was one Mark was desperate to make. "When Tony got in touch I had no hesitation in saying yes. I knew Tony had a strong affinity for Scotland from his time spent here, and I have always had a healthy respect for Scottish football. In addition, we were both very keen to progress into management, and so the opportunity to come to a big Scottish Club like Hibernian was too good to pass up."

So what qualities does Mark bring? "The players expect much the same from me as they get from the Manager – an honest approach and an open approach. They get the truth – even if it hurts sometimes."

And Mark's aims for the future? "Success for us is to improve season on season, in terms of results and performances, and to close the gap with the Old Firm. If we can do that, and we play the right football and do the right things, then we can bring more people to fill our ground."

Mark Venus – first-team coach/ player

Born: 4 June 1967 in Hartlepool Mark enjoyed an illustrious playing career as a cultured central defender in the English leagues, with former Clubs including Wolves, Leicester and Ipswich.

# Season Review

## 2004-05

### JULY

Pre-season friendlies and a brief foray into the Intertoto mark the beginning of Tony Mowbray's reign as Manager at Hibernian. A youthful squad that was to be significantly bolstered in the weeks following drew 1-1 with Lithuanians FK Vetra at Easter Road, and lost by the only goal in the away leg to depart the Intertoto competition. Better was to follow, with pre-season friendly wins scored against Berwick Rangers, Cowdenbeath, Cardiff City and Forfar before losing to a strong and experienced Leeds United side 3-1 at Easter Road.

## AUGUST

The SPL season kicked off with a home fixture against Kilmarnock. Despite suffering a 0-1 reversal, the game contained positive signs for the Easter Road fans that the new Manager's belief in an exciting passing game was worth persevering with. More battling qualities were needed for the next fixture, away to Motherwell, when two Garry O'Connor goals gained the points in a hard-fought 2-1 win which saw two Hibernian players – Brebner and Murdock – given their marching orders. A defeat to Rangers at Ibrox by 4 goals to 1 followed with Caldwell netting for the Hibees. A home fixtures then brought Alloa to Easter Road in the CIS Cup, which Hibernian won 4-0 thanks to goals from Glass, Orman, Murdock and Riordan. The final fixture of the month was a thriller, with Hibernian going behind at Easter Road to an early goal from Dundee before playing football that had opposition manager Jim Duffy drooling to force a 4-1 lead. At that stage Hibernian were cruising, but more drama was to follow as a late collapse saw Dundee net three times to force a 4-4 draw that felt more like a defeat to the green-and-white legions.

## SEPTEMBER

The Festival Cup was the first fixture of the month, with Hearts running out 3-1 winners at Tynecastle in this friendly, Dobbie scoring for Hibernian. League business took pride of place thereafter, with Hibernian scoring a solid 2-1 away win against Inverness, thanks to two Derek Riordan strikes. A thrilling 2-2 draw with Celtic followed at Easter Road, with Hibernian's goals coming through a Bobo Balde og and a super run and strike by full-back David Murphy. Hibernian twice forced the lead, and were twice pegged back by Celtic in a match that had fans and critics alike raving at the fluency of the young Hibernian side in a top class first half performance. A workmanlike 3-1 defeat of Albion Rovers in the CIS Cup was next up, with Dobbie, Shiels and O'Connor all netting, and Derek Riordan was back amongst the goals in the 1-0 defeat of Aberdeen at Pittodrie – the first time the Dons had conceded in open play.

# OCTOBER

A month of mixed fortunes in October kicked off with an away draw against Dunfermline, a Garry O'Connor goal putting the Hibernian ahead before a late equaliser saw the chance to take all three points vanish. A strong 2-0 home win against Dundee United was next up, with goals from O'Connor and Fletcher followed by the first "real" derby of the season against Hearts at Tynecastle, following a run of six SPL matches undefeated for the men from Easter Road. Sadly, a narrow defeat was the outcome despite a strong second-half showing in which Derek Riordan pulled back a goal to reduce the deficit to 2-1. A return to winning ways was to follow, with a 2-1 win against Livingston at Easter Road courtesy of goals from Beuzelin and Fletcher. The month ended weakly, with a poor showing away to Kilmarnock rewarded with a 3-1 defeat, the consolation scored by Shiels.

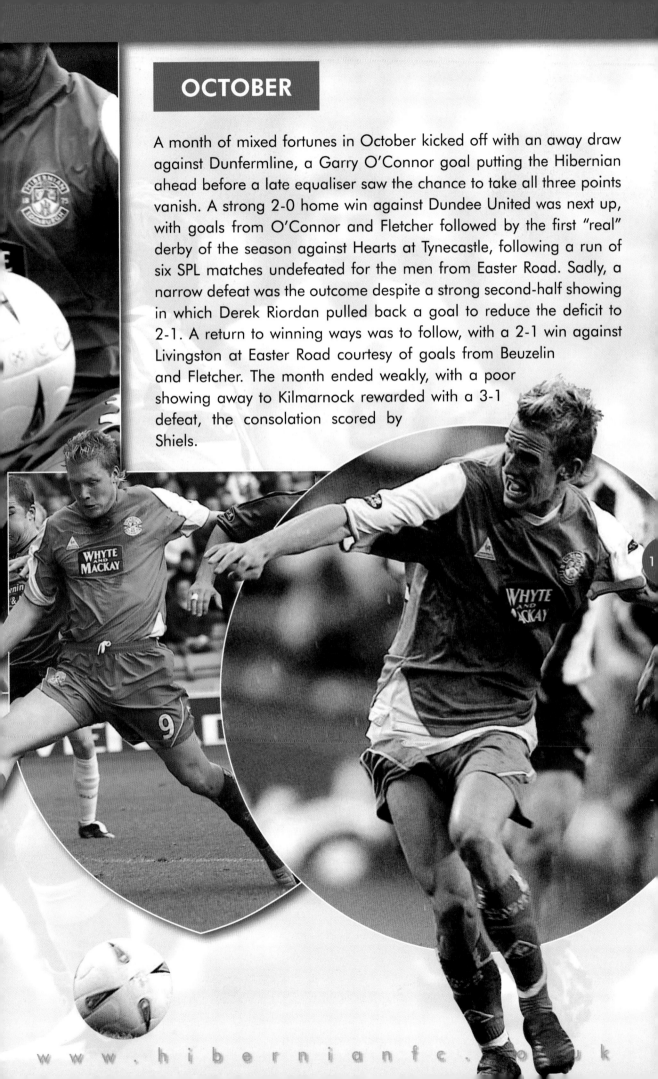

## NOVEMBER

Motherwell were first to come calling to Easter Road in November, and a flicked header from Ian Murray was enough to secure a 1-0 win and gain all three points for Hibernian. The Quarter Final of the CIS Cup against Dundee United at Tannadice was next up, and following a strong run of form Hibernian were fancied to make the semi final. It was not to be, despite a Riordan goal providing an early lead Hibernian conceded twice late in the game to crash out of the competition. A defeat by the single goal to Rangers in a thrilling Easter Road contest in which the Easter Road side did more than enough to merit taking points from the fixture followed. Dundee were put to the sword in thrilling style in a swashbuckling away win at Dens, with goals from Beuzelin, Riordan, Orman and Shiels ensuring Hibernian came back down the road with three points in a 4-1 win and Inverness were seen off 2-1 at Easter Road, despite mounting a strong challenge, through goals by Beuzelin and Riordan.

6

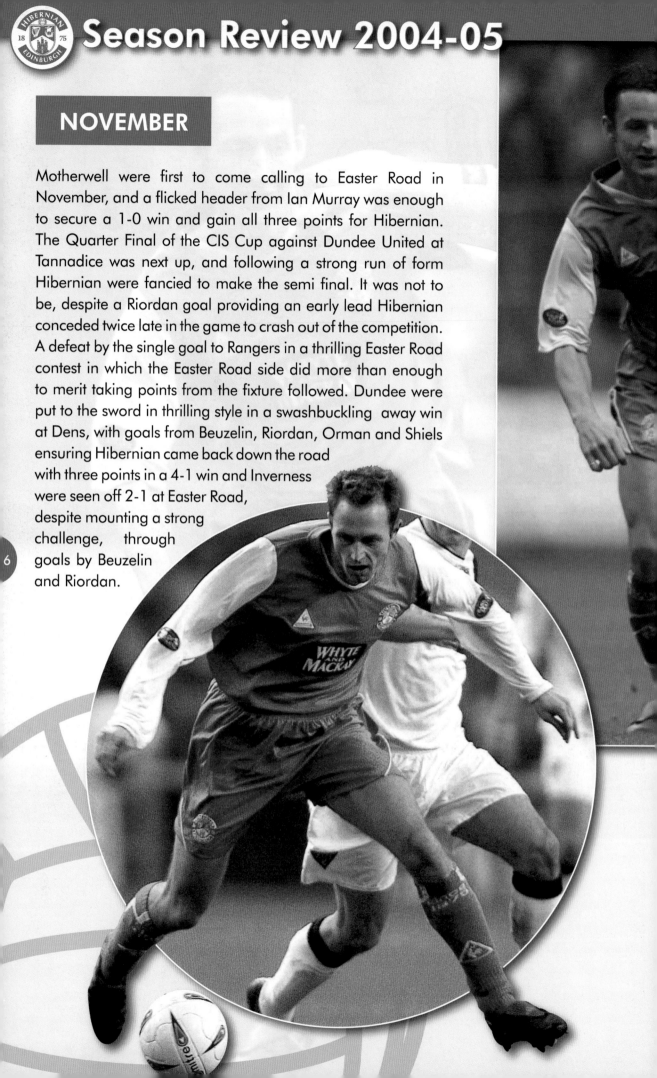

## DECEMBER

Hibernian were about to hit a three-month purple patch of form that consolidated their position as the "best of the rest" chasing Rangers and Celtic in the SPL. A scintillating passing display at Parkhead against champions Celtic ended with a 2-1 defeat as Celtic struck twice – first to take the lead and then cancel out Gary Caldwell's equaliser. Nonetheless, pundits including the Celtic management team conceded that Hibernian had played the better football and deserved more from the game. Aberdeen came calling on December 11th, needing a win to take them 10 points clear of Mowbray's men. A packed Easter Road saw Hibernian triumph in a tight and thrilling 2-1 win with goals from Derek Riordan and a memorable winning volley from Stephen Glass securing the points – and narrowing the gap between Aberdeen in third and Hibernian in fourth to just four points. Dunfermline were next up at Easter Road, with goals from Riordan and Glass again securing the three points in another 2-1 win. Hibernian ended the month with another trip to Tannadice to face Dundee United. Revenge for the CIS Cup defeat was taken in a 4-1 mauling of the men in tangerine, the goals coming from Riordan, O'Connor, Orman and Morrow.

## JANUARY

An unbeaten month was to unfold. The second derby of the season saw Hearts come to Easter Road, with the green-and-white side of the City confident of a win. It all appeared to be going to plan as Hibernian outplayed their Capital rivals in a thrilling first half in which a goal from Riordan separated the sides. However it was Hearts who started the second-half the stronger, and it was no surprise when they secured an equaliser. In a thrilling finish, Hibernian had many chances to secure all three points but failed to capitalise, and the game ended a draw. Those were the last points Hibernian dropped that month. Dundee were seen off 2-0 in the Scottish Cup at Easter Road through strikes from Whittaker and Morrow, and then Hibernian returned from a visit to Livingston with the points after goals from O'Connor and Riordan went unanswered. Kilmarnock, who had twice beaten Hibernian, were next to arrive at Easter Road but the young Hibernian side ran out comfortable 3-0 winners through a stunning Riordan hat-trick. Hibernian wrapped up the January transfer window with three new arrivals – Chris Hogg from Ipswich, Amadou Konte from Cambridge United and Ivan Sproule from Irish side Institute. Colin Murdock went in the other direction, leaving Easter Road for Crewe.

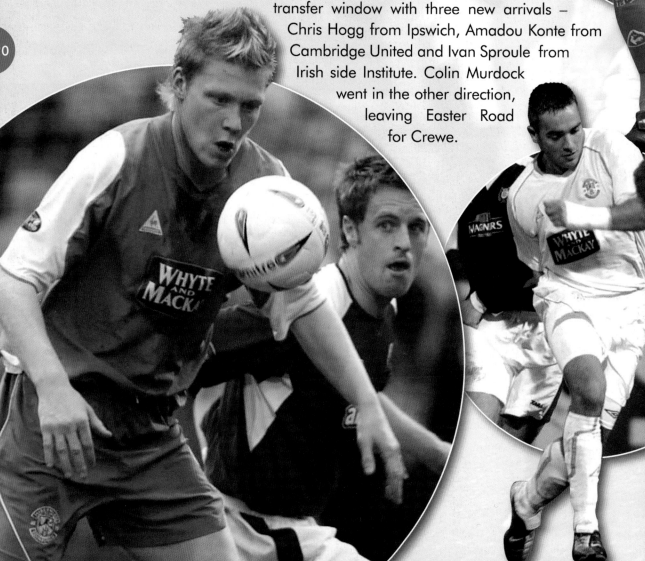

## FEBRUARY

Two goals from Garry O'Connor and strikes from Morrow and Caldwell saw Hibernian see off a spirited Brechin City 4-0 in a Scottish Cup tie at Easter Road. A disappointing 3-0 defeat to Rangers at Ibrox followed, with the Glasgow side confirming after the match that the visit of the talented young Hibernian side had motivated them in similar fashion to an Old Firm tie – a compliment indeed. A Derek Riordan goal earned a share of the points in an away match with Motherwell, and two goals from O'Connor and goals from Whittaker and Fletcher saw Dundee trounced 4-0 in the league at Easter Road. Despite the yawning scoreline, the game was never straightforward with Dundee missing a few chances of their own. The month ended with a home match against St Mirren in the Scottish Cup Quarter Final, which ended 2-0 Hibernian following goals from Scott Brown and O'Connor.

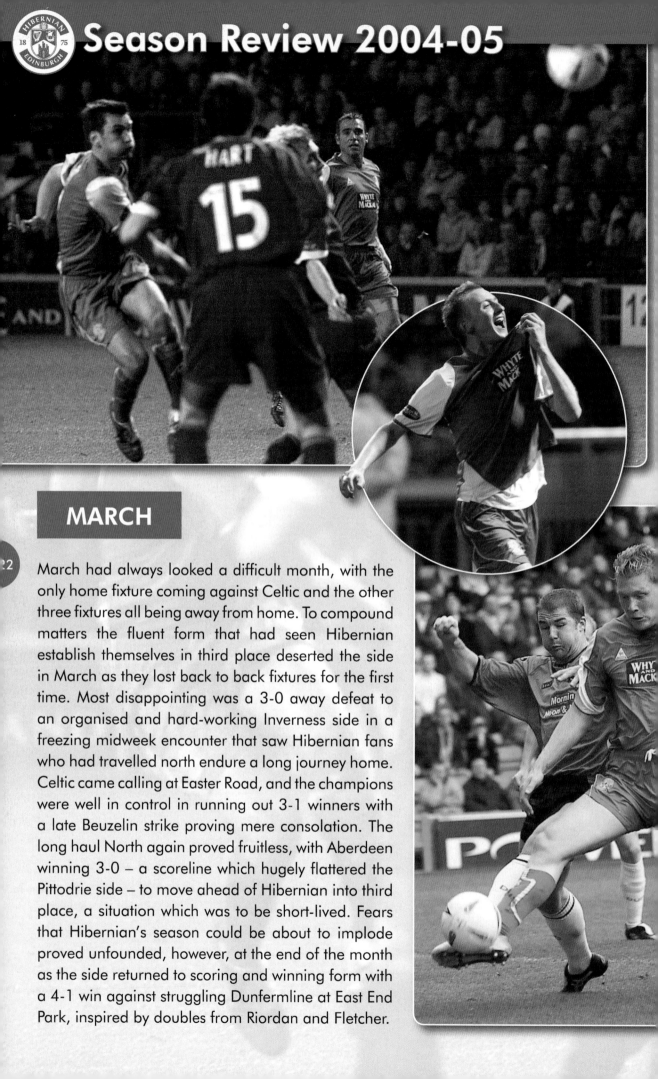

## MARCH

March had always looked a difficult month, with the only home fixture coming against Celtic and the other three fixtures all being away from home. To compound matters the fluent form that had seen Hibernian establish themselves in third place deserted the side in March as they lost back to back fixtures for the first time. Most disappointing was a 3-0 away defeat to an organised and hard-working Inverness side in a freezing midweek encounter that saw Hibernian fans who had travelled north endure a long journey home. Celtic came calling at Easter Road, and the champions were well in control in running out 3-1 winners with a late Beuzelin strike proving mere consolation. The long haul North again proved fruitless, with Aberdeen winning 3-0 – a scoreline which hugely flattered the Pittodrie side – to move ahead of Hibernian into third place, a situation which was to be short-lived. Fears that Hibernian's season could be about to implode proved unfounded, however, at the end of the month as the side returned to scoring and winning form with a 4-1 win against struggling Dunfermline at East End Park, inspired by doubles from Riordan and Fletcher.

A dramatic month of highs and lows began with a thrilling 3-2 home win against a recovering Dundee United side. Hibernian twice went ahead through goals by Shiels and O'Connor, and twice were pegged back. A draw looked inevitable until Hibernian scored a last-gasp winner through the unlikely source of Gary Smith. Dundee United did not have long to wait for revenge, the Tannadice men were next up at Hampden for the Scottish Cup semi-final. All went according to plan for the first 70 minutes, but a lone Riordan penalty was not added to – despite numerous chances – and as the game wore on an edgy Hibernian lost their fluency and United scored twice to make the Final. A derby match against arch-rivals Hearts at Tynecastle provided the perfect opportunity to exorcise the ghosts, but the signs looked bad as Hibernian fell behind and put in a stuttering first half performance. The second half was an entirely different affair, and the men in green and white dominated the match and

scored twice to take all three points and send their fans home delirious. Livingston, struggling to avoid relegation, were expected to be disposed of easily at Easter Road but a combination of a sluggish Hibernian performance and a disciplined Livi display saw the Lions win 3-0 to shock Hibernian. Following the SPL split, with Hibernian firmly in the top 6, Hearts again came calling to Easter Road eager to avenge their defeat just a fortnight earlier. In a thrilling match before a full house, the game ended with a late Hearts equaliser in a 2-2 draw, with Hibernian netting through O'Connor and Riordan. Undoubtedly the highlight for many fans was to follow, as Hibernian travelled to Parkhead to tackle champions and leaders Celtic. A superb display of counter-attacking with pace saw Hibernian stun Celtic 3-1, the goals coming from O'Connor, Sproule and Brown.

23

# Season Review 2004-05

## MAY

Aberdeen were breathing down Hibernian necks in the race for third spot and the UEFA Cup place. A difficult visit to Motherwell was first up, and Hibernian looked to be down and out with less than 15 minutes remaining at 0-2. However a superb free kick from Gary Caldwell revitalised the team, and a late scrambed equaliser from Amadou Konte gained a share of the spoils that could have been more if the game had gone on a further few minutes. How vital that last gasp goal was to prove. Aberdeen came calling, six points behind with two games to play and an inferior goal difference. Only a win would suffice for the Dons, and any point would see Hibernian claim third place. Another full house saw a thrilling match which Aberdeen won 2-1, with Riordan scoring for Hibernian. Aberdeen were three points behind, with Hibernian enjoying a superior goal difference of five. The stage was set for an incredible end to the season, with Hibernian entertaining Rangers – chasing an outside chance of an SPL title and knowing they had to win and hope Celtic slipped up at Motherwell. Aberdeen, meantime, were at home to a massively weakened Hearts side knowing they had to win and score as many as possible into the bargain. As news filtered through from Pittodrie that Aberdeen had taken a

| Top Scorers 04/05 | Goals (all competitions) | Appearances |
|---|---|---|
| Derek Riordan | 23 | 43 |
| Garry O'Connor | 19 | 42 |
| Dean Shiels | 6 | 42 |
| Steven Fletcher | 5 | 26 |
| Guillaume Beuzelin | 4 | 29 |
| Gary Caldwell | 4 | 46 |
| Stephen Glass | 3 | 44 |
| Alen Orman | 3 | 18 |
| Sam Morrow | 3 | 28 |
| Steven Whittaker | 2 | 45 |
| Scott Brown | 2 | 24 |
| Amadou Konte | 1 | 13 |
| Ivan Sproule | 1 | 9 |
| Gary Smith | 1 | 24 |
| Ian Murray | 1 | 33 |
| David Murphy | 1 | 32 |
| Stephen Dobbie | 1 | 12 |
| Colin Murdock | 1 | 9 |

lead, most fans were unconcerned as the minutes ticked by with the game at Easter Road locked at 0-0. Celtic had taken an early lead against Motherwell, and the title appeared to be heading to Parkhead. Rangers scored into the second half when a scrambled Novo shot was deflected by Gary Caldwell to give the 'Gers fans something to cheer about. Aberdeen scored again, to take a 2-0 lead, and the goal difference was down to 2. Then came the news that had Rangers fans dancing – Motherwell had snatched a late equaliser and the destination of the title had swung to Ibrox. Further jubilation followed as Motherwell grabbed a last-gasp winner to assure Rangers of the title. Aberdeen were unable to add to their total, and the Hibernian fans joined in the celebrations as word filtered through that Tony Mowbray's green-and-white Army would enjoy a European excursion the following season.

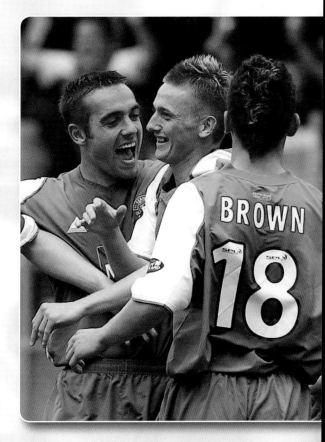

## Scottish Premier League - Season 2004/2005 - Final Table

| | P | W | D | L | F | A | GD | Pts |
|---|---|---|---|---|---|---|---|---|
| Rangers | 38 | 28 | 6 | 4 | 78 | 22 | +56 | 93 |
| Celtic | 38 | 30 | 2 | 6 | 85 | 35 | +50 | 92 |
| Hibernian | 38 | 18 | 7 | 13 | 64 | 57 | +7 | 61 |
| Aberdeen | 38 | 18 | 7 | 13 | 44 | 39 | +5 | 61 |
| Hearts | 38 | 13 | 11 | 14 | 43 | 41 | +2 | 50 |
| Motherwell | 38 | 13 | 9 | 16 | 46 | 49 | -3 | 48 |
| | | | | | | | | |
| Kilmarnock | 38 | 15 | 4 | 19 | 49 | 54 | -5 | 49 |
| Inverness C.T. | 38 | 11 | 11 | 16 | 40 | 46 | -6 | 44 |
| Dundee United | 38 | 8 | 12 | 18 | 40 | 58 | -18 | 36 |
| Livingston | 38 | 9 | 8 | 21 | 34 | 62 | -28 | 35 |
| Dunfermline | 38 | 8 | 10 | 20 | 33 | 60 | -26 | 34 |
| Dundee | 38 | 8 | 9 | 21 | 38 | 70 | -32 | 33 |

26

# Hibernian Quiz

## QUIZ A: Who Said That?

Can you identify which Hibernian players, coaches or directors made the following remarks during the course of last season? Watch out for the non-Hibee quote. Answers on page 61...

1. " I was at Middlesbrough at the same time as Phil Stamp – so I'm looking forward to meeting him again. "

2. " I prefer playing football as opposed to running about, especially hard training. "

3. " Every international cap I've had has been while playing at Hibernian... "

4. " Deek sets me up; I set him up. "

5. " I don't really think about being the oldest in the team, playing in the position I'm in you already have a responsibility to communicate and organise things. "

6. " Our aim before kick-off today was simply to qualify for Europe. "

7. " The doctor realigned my back and that relieved the pressure on my ankle! The doctor just realigned the equilibrium of my body a bit! "

8. " I can play for Scotland as my dad is from Cumnock and hopefully I can get a call-up. I would love to play for them, I was born in England but have never represented them at any level. My mum is Italian and my dad moved south when he was five, so I have never set foot in Scotland until I joined Hibernian! "

9. " I don't know how much Celtic know about Ivan - but the boy is electrically quick, and he managed to get us up the pitch and cause them problems after the pace had gone out of the game. "

10. " At the start of the second half Hibernian were exceptional. I know the Hibernian fans will not be happy losing a 4-1 lead but if they play that type of football for sustained periods then Hibernian will have a good season. "

# Hibernian in Europe

It was fitting that season 2004/05 should end with Hibernian qualifying for European competition through a third-place finish in the league and a slot in the UEFA Cup draw.

Because 50 years earlier, in 1955, Hibernian became the first British Club to compete in European competition when they were invited to compete in the inaugural Champions Cup. The great Hibernian side of The Famous Five was drawn against German cracks Rott Weiss Essen – a side that contained several members of that nation's World Cup winning team of 1954.

Hibernian won the first leg, away from home, 4-0. As Eddie Turnbull described it "we gassed them, although they were not a bad team." Eddie himself scored the first goal – and achieved immortality as the first British player to score in European competition. The return leg finished 1-1, with Hibernian through 5-1 on aggregate.

Defeat in the competition came at the semi-final stage, when French champions Reims inspired by the great footballer Raymond Kopa beat Hibernian 3-0 on aggregate. Lawrie Reilly, another of The Famous Five, commented: "He was the best player I have played against. He was brilliant, and without him we would have beaten Reims and gone to meet Real Madrid in the final."

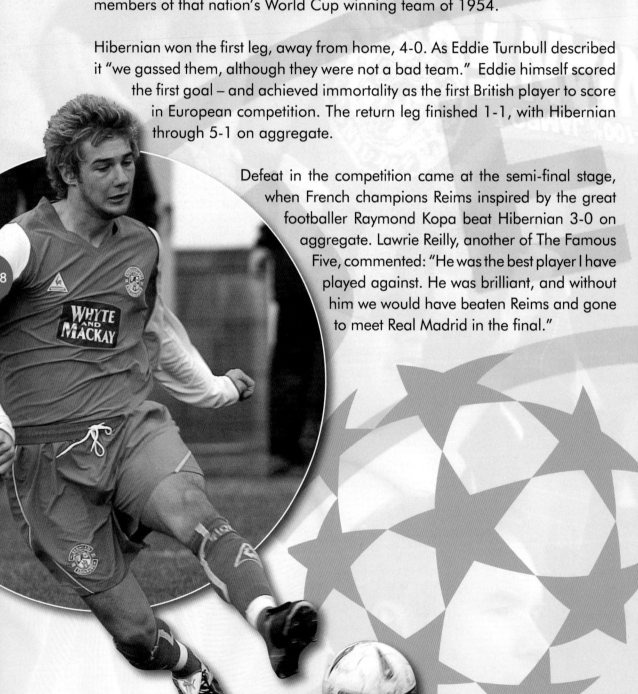

By that stage, The Famous Five were past their prime, a fact often lamented by the great Gordon Smith who said: "The big regret I have about that team is that the European Cup didn't start till the mid '50s. If it had been in the early '50s I am convinced Hibernian would have won it. The two years we won the league we were an outstanding team who could have beaten anyone."

Further great sorties into Europe were to follow, however. In particular, a pulsating and unforgettable 7-6 aggregate defeat of Barcelona in 1960/61 in the then Fairs Cup (now UEFA Cup). Hibernian had come away with a 4-4 draw in the Nou Camp to take home to Easter Road. All did not go according to plan, with the Catalans taking a half-time lead of 2-1 – a lead they held until the 74th minute when Tommy Preston headed home an equaliser. With five minutes to go, Hibernian were awarded a penalty when John McLeod was fouled – unleashing a storm of protest from the Barcelona players that threatened to ruin the game. Bobby Kinloch tucked away the spot kick to give Hibernian a memorable victory over one of the game's giants.

As well as the result, those who witnessed the match also can't forget the mayhem. Joe Baker recalled: "You had to be there to believe it." He added: "Barcelona had gone totally crazy." Policemen and Hibernian players had to help protect the referee and linesman from the Barca players when the final whistle sounded.

# Hibernian in Europe

That took Hibernian to a semi-final meeting with Italian greats AS Roma, which ended with an aggregate score of 5-5 following two draws. In those days a third match was ordered to determine the matter – and remarkably it was played in Rome. Hibernian went out.

The next major milestone came in season 1967-68, when Hibernian met Napoli in the second round of the Fairs Cup and Hibernian were thumped 4-1 in the away leg. The return at Easter Road looked a formality, and so the Italians thought. But on Wednesday, November 29, 1967 Hibernian recorded one of the amazing European comebacks thumping the Italians 5-0 to go through to meet Don Revie's Leeds United in a quarter final which was lost by the narrowest of margins, 2-1 on aggregate.

There have been other great adventures – notably the 7-2 aggregate hammering of Sporting Lisbon in 1972-73 which included a second-leg hat-trick from Jimmy O'Rourke, and a 12-3 thrashing of Norwegians Rosenborg in 1974-75 which seems incredible to us today. In that game, Pat Stanton scored two.

Our most recent escapade in the major European competitions came in season 2000-2001, when the Club faced a tricky task against Greek club AEK Athens – a team which regularly reaches the quarter final stages of the competitions and qualifies for the Champions League.

A 2-0 away defeat meant the side faced a huge task at Easter Road. In the finest Hibernian spirit, Alex McLeish's side came back to win 2-0 and level the scores after 90 minutes, both goals from Spanish striker Paco Luna. The same player missed a golden opportunity to head the winner in the 90th minute. It was to prove a costly miss, as the Greeks scored twice in extra-time to kill the tie, despite a magnificent David Zitelli strike winning the home tie 3-2 for Hibernian.

In all, Hibernian have qualified for Europe on 18 occasions, including this season. We have won more ties than we have lost, suffering defeats in only 1 in 3 of our appearances on average. In terms of Scottish standing in Europe, our record is eclipsed only by the Old Firm, Aberdeen and Dundee United.

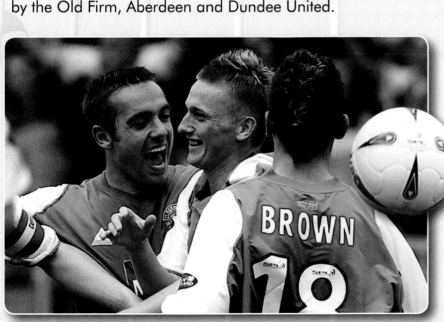

# Garry O'Connor
## Player Interview

Garry O'Connor was a regular star performer for Hibernian during last season with all-action, powerful displays that rattled every defence he came up against.

The big centre-forward's form was described by his Manager, Tony Mowbray, as awesome in more than one post-match press conference, and earned the player a recall to Scotland duty.

In all competitions he netted 19 goals – some spectacular but all of them valuable.

But it isn't just on the pitch on match days that this likeable lad sets himself targets – he's determined in the year ahead to continue making progress in all aspects of his life.

He said: " I had a good season, and I was much happier with my form. Since the gaffer has come in I've got a new lease of life, and I feel I am back to showing the kind of form I should be.

" The Manager and Mark Venus have been great with me, encouraging me every step of the way and the coaching is fantastic. I am very happy with the way things are going.

" It was good to be called back into the Scotland set-up as well, that was a real bonus and now I want to push on and play an even greater role. That means continuing to improve as a player and with Tony as my Club manager and Walter Smith at the helm of the national team I would like to think I can continue to make progress.

"I want to continue to score my share of goals, and to work hard for the team and to see us continue to improve as a team. I think last season everyone could see the big strides forward that we made under the gaffer and Mark, and everyone was excited by the style of play."

Garry was voted Player of the Year last season by the Hibernian Supporters' Association, and appreciates the backing he receives from fans.

"It makes a huge difference to the players when they know the fans are behind them, and last season was terrific everywhere we went. There were away matches where our fans outnumbered the opposition, and it was fantastic to see so many of them turn out to follow the team.

"At Easter Road, we had quite a few sell-outs, and that was also great to see. The atmosphere that generates is fantastic to play in, and it really gives us a lift. There's no doubt that our attacking play has captured the fans' imaginations."

## So of his 19 goals, does Garry have a favourite?

" It's hard to pick one favourite, but scoring twice against Hearts and one against Celtic at Parkhead must be the short list. The goals against Hearts were great because it's the derby and it matters so much to the fans and to us. The first at Tynecastle in April got us back into the game after a poor first half, and Dean Shiels then got a terrific winner. The second came against Hearts at Easter Road two weeks later, and gave us the lead.

"The Celtic goal was the best of the three in terms of quality of goal, I think. Derek (Riordan) gave a terrific back-heel pass to Scott (Brown) who ran half the length of the park with the ball before he slipped a nice wee pass to me. I turned Stan Varga and slotted it in the corner, and it silenced Parkhead – apart from the Hibernian fans who went wild – as it put us a goal up in the first few minutes."

# Garry's Goals

## Game by Game 2004-05

### Hibernian v FK Vetra, Intertoto Cup, July 3rd

**Goal 1:** The match was played at a soaking Easter Road. With just 15 minutes left, and Hibernian a goal behind, Stephen Glass produced a superb pass to Garry – in space in an area of the pitch that wasn't waterlogged –and he used the good purchase to turn the Vetra defence and send the ball low into the corner.

### Motherwell v Hibernian, SPL, August 14th

**Goals 2 and 3:** A two goal performance from Garry. The first came from a superb through ball from Grant Brebner in the first half which saw Garry shrug off challenges from two defenders and slip the ball past the advancing goalie.

Motherwell equalised, and Hibernian had to wait until the 77th minute to get the winner, Garry getting on the end of a deep cross from Sam Morrow to acrobatically tip the ball in to the top corner.

### Hibernian v Dundee, SPL, August 28th

**Goals 4 and 5:** A dramatic 4-4 draw after Hibernian had taken a 4-1 lead and appeared to be cruising to a stylish victory. Garry's goal came in the 47th minute, latching onto a long ball, rounding the keeper and sending the ball into the corner. His second came from a glancing header a few moments later.

### Albion Rovers v Hibernian, CIS Cup, September 22nd

**Goal 6:** The second goal struck by Garry from a Dean Shiels slipped pass gave Hibernian the cushion their play had merited.

### Dunfermline v Hibernian, SPL, October 2nd

**Goal 7:** This strike came a few minutes before half-time, when Derek Riordan pushed the ball into Garry's path and he picked his spot and sent the ball into the bottom left hand corner.

### Hibernian v Dundee United, SPL, October 16th

**Goal 8:** Garry had set up Derek Riordan with an opportunity earlier in the game, and his strike partner returned the favour by teasing a defender out to him, slipping the ball into Garry who made no mistake from seven yards.

### Dundee United v Hibernian, SPL, December 27th

**Goal 9:** On 22 minutes Murphy squared to Riordan who shaped to shoot but sent a ball into the area to Orman, who knocked it down to Garry who hammered it home from 10 yards.

## Livingston v Hibernian, SPL, January 15th

**Goal 10:** Steven Whittaker made a powerful run and slipped a ball into Garry's path. His pace and power took him away from the defenders and he slotted a shot from a tight angle in 52 minutes to give Hibernian the lead.

## Hibernian v Brechin City, Scottish Cup, February 5th

**Goal 11 and 12:** Again started by a Whittaker pass to Riordan, a low ball into the area which Garry latched onto and blasted past the keeper. The goal, in the 32nd minute, doubled the Hibernian lead. Garry scored the third also when Sheils played a delightful ball right through the heart of the visiting defence and in to his path.

## Hibernian v Dundee, SPL, February 19th

**Goals 13 and 14:** Garry put Hibernian into the lead in the 28th minute after Dundee keeper Soutar had parried a Riordan strike into his path. His second – the team's fourth - came after he latched onto a pass from Antonio Murray.

## Hibernian v St Mirren, Scottish Cup QF, February 26th

**Goal 15:** A delightful long pass from Whittaker into Garry's path saw the striker race away from the defence, round the keeper and coolly slot home the team's second.

## Hibernian v Dundee United, SPL, April 2nd

**Goal 16:** A second for Hibernian in a 3-2 thriller came with just 20 minutes left when Stephen Glass played the ball to Garry who slammed a powerful shot past Tony Bullock.

## Hearts v Hibernian, SPL, April 13th

**Goal 17:** Hibernian were trailing 0-1 with less than 25 minutes to go when substitute Amadou Konte sent a looping ball into the area. Dean Shiels knocked the ball to Garry, who slipped a low shot through a sea of bodies to pull Hibernian level.

## Hibernian v Hearts, SPL, April 23rd

**Goal 18:** Hibernian took the lead when the ball was swung into the Hearts area, a clearing header went only as far as Scott Brown and his ball back into the area fell for Garry who touched it into the net.

## Celtic v Hibernian, SPL, April 30th

**Goal 19:** A delightful goal started with a cheeky back-heel from Riordan to Brown, a surging run from the midfielder and a clever little ball to Garry who turned Stan Varga before slotting into the bottom corner to set Hibernian on their way.

# Player Profiles

## Goalkeepers:

### Simon Brown – goalkeeper

Born: 3 December 1976 in Chelmsford

One of Tony Mowbray's first signings following the departure of goalies Nick Colgan and Daniel Anderson, Simon joined the Club from English league side Colchester. A burly 6ft 2in tall, Simon is an agile shot stopper and has been a regular first-team pick in league and Scottish Cup matches since making his debut in pre-season clashes with Cardiff City and Leeds United. Former clubs include Spurs, Fulham and Lincoln.

### Alistair Brown – goalkeeper

Born: 12 December 1985 in Irvine

Ally made his first-team debut in the Intertoto Cup against Lithuanian side FK Vetra after new signing Simon Brown suffered a foot injury in training. Ally has been selected for Scotland u-21 squads and is a capable and promising young keeper. He joined the Club in May 2003 from Cowdenbeath.

# Defenders:

## Gary Smith – defender

Born: 25 March 1971 in Glasgow

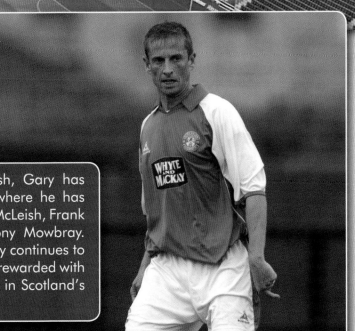

Signed by former Manager Alex McLeish, Gary has proven a shrewd signing for the Club where he has played key roles in the sides managed by McLeish, Frank Sauzee, Bobby Williamson and now Tony Mowbray. Despite reaching the "veteran" stage, Gary continues to demonstrate his value to the side and was rewarded with a further one-year contract with the Club in Scotland's top flight.

## David Murphy – defender

Born: 1 March 1983 in Hartlepool

David ended the Club's search for a left-back after impressing in a pre-season friendly against Cardiff City in July 2004. He came to the Club's attention through the Manager's Middlesbrough connections, and signed from the Premiership side on an initial two year deal. A powerful tackler, David brings strong defensive qualities to the side as well as being capable – as he has shown many times – of swashbuckling forays forward.

37

## Gary Caldwell – defender

Born: 12 April 1982 in Stirling

An experienced Scotland international, Gary brings great technical ability to his role in the centre of defence. He is also more than capable, as he has shown at international level, of performing a first-class holding midfield role. He signed for the Club on a two-year deal from Newcastle United, following earlier loan spells at Easter Road. As well as his excellent reading of the game and passing ability, Gary has shown he is adept at the other end of the pitch, in particular with free kicks.

## Steven Whittaker – defender

Born: 16 June 1984 in Edinburgh

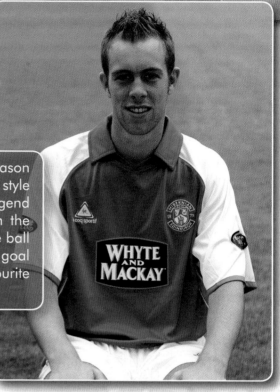

A young player who has really come of age during season 2004/05. Steven's adventurous, athletic and skilful style of play has had no less a judge than Hibernian legend Eddie Turnbull compare the young full-back with the great John Brownlie. Dangerous and pacy with the ball at his feet, Steven is not afraid to have a crack at goal when the opportunity presents itself. A firm favourite with the fans.

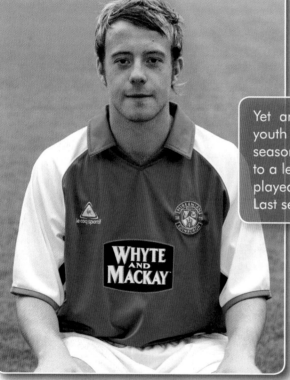

## Jonathan Baillie – defender

Born: 2 September 1985 in Irvine

Yet another product of the highly-praised Hibernian youth system, Jonathan made his first-team debut in season 2003/04 in spectacular style, helping the team to a league cup quarter final win over Celtic by 2-1. He played a key role, helping stifle the Celtic strikeforce. Last season was written off by a recurring toe injury.

## Chris Hogg – defender

Born: 12 March 1985 in Middlesbrough

Another Mowbray signing, Chris joined Hibernian from the Manager's previous Club Ipswich Town. A centre-back with great potential, Chris has represented England at various youth levels. A serious arm injury sustained while attempting to foil a car thief meant that last season was a write-off. He will be hoping to break into regular first team action and enjoy a trouble-free season.

38

## Jay Shields – defender

Born: 6 July 1985 in Edinburgh

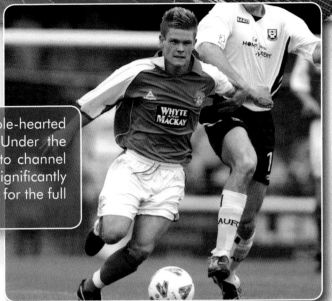

A stuffy little terrier of a player, Jay brings whole-hearted commitment and aggression to his play. Under the tutelage of Tony Mowbray, he has learned to channel these into a positive force, and has improved significantly as an all-round footballer providing back-up for the full back berths.

# Midfield:

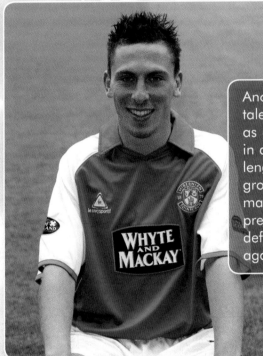

## Scott Brown – midfield

Born: 25 June 1985 in Fife

Another fine example of the production line of young talent at Easter Road – Scott's skills seem to increase as each month goes by and last season he impressed in a mature midfield role following his recovery from a lengthy injury. Scott has a fantastic ability to cover the ground, can score with either foot, and is capable of making exciting and dangerous runs – but he is also prepared to work for the team and doesn't neglect his defensive duties. Season capped by a memorable goal against Celtic at Parkhead.

## Guillaume Beuzelin – midfield

Born: 14 April 1979 in Le Havre, France

A quality midfield player skilled on either foot and with a superb first touch, Guillaume is an integral part of Tony Mowbray's determination to play passing, attacking football. His ability to make the best use of space and to see a pass early has been a major source of excitement around Easter Road. And he can score, as well. Keeping his trial period quiet to avoid attracting the interests of others was a Mowbray master stroke when Guillaume joined from Le Havre!

## Kevin Thomson – midfield

Born: 16 January 1983
in Edinburgh

The roar that greeted Kevin's Easter Road return after a year spent injured was testament to the affection that this talented young player is held in. He established himself in the first team in season 2003/04, but unhappily a serious knee injury ruled out much of last season for this midfield play-maker. A real talent, with a gifted left-foot all Hibernian fans will be hoping that with the benefit of a full pre-season behind him Kevin can pick up where he left off two seasons ago.

## Dean Shiels – midfield/striker

Born: 1 February 1985
in Northern Ireland

Dean has been one of the finds of last season – a real revelation. Signed from Arsenal the youngster took little time to settle in Edinburgh and exceeded all expectations – including the Manager's! Originally taken on as a back-up striker, Dean demonstrated his versatility throughout the season by establishing himself as a non-stop and skilful midfield player.

## Stephen Glass – midfield/ defender

Born: 23 May 1976
in Dundee

A left-sided player of real quality, Stephen suffered from an injury-hit first season on moving to Hibernian at the start of season 2003/04 from Watford. However, a run in the team last season saw his undoubted ability shine through. He played a key role in both midfield and, when required, at full-back. One highlight was an outstanding volleyed goal against closest rivals Aberdeen in a vital match at Easter Road. Former Clubs include Aberdeen and Newcastle United.

## Ivan Sproule – midfield

Born: 18 February 1981
in Omagh, Northern Ireland

Blistering pace persuaded Tony Mowbray to take a chance on Ivan, who joined Hibernian from Irish side Institute. The winger took little time to settle, and has quickly demonstrated the potential that persuaded the Manager, scoring a fantastic goal against Celtic at Parkhead and sparking a vital late revival in an away match against Motherwell. Ivan looks set to provide many moments of excitement for Easter Road fans.

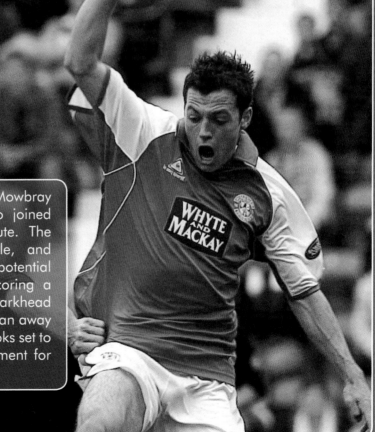

## Jamie McCluskey – midfield

Born: 6 November 1987
in Bellshill

"Jinky" is blessed with the kind of trickery and skills that fans love to see. A lively, talented little player he has enjoyed several first team outings and has shown his huge potential. Undoubtedly the best is still to come from this star in the making – a prospect that has Hibees salivating in anticipation.

## Antonio Murray – midfield

Born: 15 September 1984
in Cambridge

Antonio was signed during the January transfer window last year from Ipswich Town, where he was on the fringes of first team squad action. The son of Italian and Scottish parents, brought up in England's south east, he was thrown into the hurly-burly of SPL action faster than he or the coaching staff anticipated due to a spate of injuries to other midfield players, and came through with flying colours. He has a decent touch, strong shot and is fearless in the tackle.

## Kevin Nicol – midfield

Born: 19 January 1982
in Kirkcaldy

Kevin was signed from Raith Rovers during Frank Sauzee's tenure, although he had been identified as a target during Alex McLeish's reign at Easter Road. He enjoyed his best spell in season 2003/04, when he enjoyed a regular run in the first-team squad which was ended by a lengthy injury. Currently on loan in Norway, Kevin is hoping to force his way back into contention.

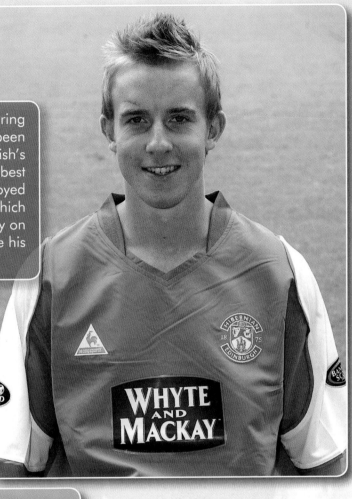

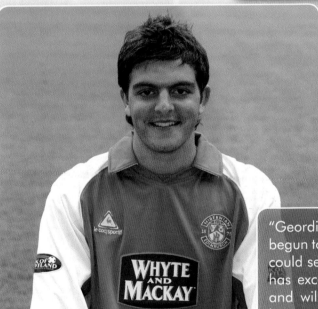

## Kevin McDonald – midfield

Born: 26 June 1985
in Newcastle-upon-Tyne

"Geordie" is a talented young footballer who has begun to show the signs of maturity in his game that could see him develop into a first-team regular. He has excellent passing ability and can score goals and will be hoping that this is the season when he can make the breakthrough as so many other Hibernian youngsters have done.

# Strikers:

## Garry O'Connor – striker

Born: 7 May 1983 in Edinburgh

Garry first exploded onto the scene at the age of just 17 – leading to his selection for the full international side very early in his career. Then came a slump in form, with Garry playing a target striker role under former manager Bobby Williamson. Perhaps the most-improved player under Tony Mowbray, Garry was back to his awesome best last season and forced his way back into the international set-up – not only through his 19 goal haul but also through his all-round game. A powerful and pacy centre-forward, Garry has been tireless and unselfish and has played like a man re-born for the new management team.

44

## Derek Riordan – striker

Born: 16 January 1983 in Edinburgh

Derek underlined his claim to be the most exciting young talent in Scotland last season when his haul of 23 goals was the highest by a Scot in the SPL – and topped only by Old Firm duo John Hartson and Nacho Novo. Derek's goals included few tap ins – and plenty of spectacular efforts. His partnership with long-time team mate and friend Garry O'Connor was a key reason behind the Club's successful season, with their contrasting styles providing defenders with many headaches.

## Sam Morrow – striker

Born: 3 March 1985 in Londonderry, Northern Ireland

Signed in the summer of 2004 from Ipswich Town, Tony Mowbray described the signing of Sam as "opportune." The youngster has shown plenty of appetite to be involved in the first-team although his appearances were limited by the form of Riordan and O'Connor. Sam has shown a keen eye for goal and a willingness to take on defenders that promises much.

## Steven Fletcher – striker

Born: 26 March 1987 in Shrewsbury

The tall teenage striker has had critics and fans alike drooling over the quality of his performances for the first-team – when asked to play up front or in a midfield role. His non-stop style and his ability on the ball mark him out as a young player with the ability to make it at the very top and Steven will be hoping to make an even bigger impact this season.

45

## Amadou Konte – striker

Born: 23 January 1981 in Mali

A quick, strong centre-forward Amadou Konte added some real physical presence to Hibernian's goal threat when he signed in January 2005 from Cambridge United. A towering 6ft 3in tall, he has also played at Strasbourg and at FC Porto, Villanovense (in Spain) and in Italy at Serie C1 side Paterno Calcio.

# Know Your History?

## Some highlights from our history

Hibernian FC was founded in 1875 by members of the Catholic Young Men's Society attached to St Patrick's Church in Edinburgh's "Little Ireland" – the Cowgate – with the blessing of Canon Edward Hannan as an amateur charitable football club.

The name – decided on by Father Hannan and the Club's first captain and co-founder Michael Whelahan – derives from the Latin and means Irishmen.

Playing in green and white, with the harp as its emblem, the Club quickly established a reputation for its play, and indeed won the Scottish Cup in 1887 thanks to a 2-1 win over Dumbarton. A defeat of Preston North End in a challenge match the same year saw the Club crowned "World Club Champions".

However as a Catholics only club in its early years, and with its roots firmly embedded in the city's poverty-stricken Irish immigrant community, Hibernian faced deep-seated resentment and open hostility from the footballing establishment in Scotland and the Club's acceptance into the Scottish Football Association, in 1887, was far from smooth.

Worse was to follow. In helping a club with similar roots, Glasgow Celtic, become established Hibernian suffered as the Glasgow side stripped Hibernian of a core of players. The Edinburgh side faced extinction in 1891 and only the intervention of a stalwart group including one Philip Farmer, great grand uncle of current principal shareholder Sir Tom Farmer CBE, saved the Club in its hour of need and Hibernian was reborn as a Club open to all.

Celtic are not, however, the only Scottish senior side to owe a debt of gratitude to Hibernian. In 1909, Hibernian played in a friendly to help launch a side amongst the Irish immigrant community in Dundee – then called Dundee Hibernian. The side were later to gain greater game as Dundee United.

Romance has always played a key role in the history of Hibernian – in terms of the flowing and attacking nature of play favoured by the Club and its supporters and also in terms of the Club's innovation and ground-breaking traditions.

For example, Hibernian was the first British Club to play in European competition in season 1955/56, the first to play under floodlights and to install under-soil heating and – in the 1980s – broke the mould by allowing shirt sponsorship.

Great periods of success have blossomed throughout the Club's history –Championships delivered in 1902/03 and in 1947/48 with a further two in 1950/51 and again the following season – the peak of powers of the Club's most celebrated team dominated by arguably the greatest forward line the British domestic game has seen, "The Famous Five."

The Scottish game's other major prize, the Scottish Cup, has been won only twice – first of all in 1887 courtesy of a 2-1 win over Dumbarton and again in 1902 in a 1-0 win over Celtic.

Greater success has been achieved in the League Cup, with wins in 1972/73 and again in 1991/92.

The first of these wins was achieved during the Club's second golden era – that of Turnbull's Tornadoes. Eddie Turnbull, one of the lauded "Famous Five" along with Smith, Johnstone, Reilly and Ormond, returned to Hibernian from Aberdeen where he had piloted the Dons to Scottish Cup success. Turnbull constructed a side vaunted all over for its flair and ability, and during his tenure the Club was to win the League Cup and two Drybrough Cups. The haul would undoubtedly have been greater, had that side not been playing at the same time as the great "9-ina-row" Celtic team of Jock Stein.

Between 1979 and 1989 Hibernian enjoyed little success and missed out on European competition. This lean period, however, was enlivened by the signing of former European Footballer of the Year, George Best, for two seasons and the former Manchester United star attracted thousands to watch Hibernian' matches.

In 1990, Wallace Mercer of city rivals Heart of Midlothian staged a controversial attempt to take-over the Club, which was in financial melt-down. Sir Tom Farmer CBE saved the Club in 1991 when its owner, the listed company Forth Investments plc, went into receivership.

After two years of turmoil, the new stability brought to the Club paid immediate dividends to the fans when Hibernian won the 1991 Skol League Cup, beating Rangers in the semi finals (1-0) and Dunfermline in the final (2-0).

In the mid 1990s developments off the field saw the building of two new stands giving Easter Road an all covered capacity of 16,000 seats, and at the turn of the decade we witnessed a landmark moment in the Club's history as we bid farewell to the famous Easter Road slope, and the construction of a magnificent new main stand.

# Youth Academy

Hibernian has rightly been praised for giving exciting young talent an opportunity to shine – but the conveyor belt that has brought through gifted young players in recent years is no accident.

The Hibernian youth system is the responsibility of the hard-working John Park, The Hibernian Academy Director, and one of the few people working in Scotland to have successfully completed the FA Academy Director's qualification.

John oversees a network of coaches and scouts that covers Scotland and he himself has a network of contacts and scouts throughout England and even further afield. During his time at the helm he has been proud to see young stars like Derek Riordan, Garry O'Connor, Steven Whittaker, Ian Murray, Scott Brown and Kevin Thompson come through to become regulars in the first team.

Prior to joining up at Easter Road John worked at Motherwell, where he helped develop the careers of James McFadden, Lee McCulloch, Steve Craigan and Steve Hammell.

Along with his team of coaches John runs coaching sessions throughout the central belt. Almost any night of the year, the Club is involved in running a youth session at some location.

He said: " A lot of people do a lot of work to ensure our youth system performs well. Our emphasis at this Club is on giving youth its chance, and that makes it easier for us to attract good young players."

John works with a number of colleagues on the SFA steering group on youth development, and believes more and more clubs are now determined to ensure a supply of high quality young players. "That bodes well for the game and for our national team."

He works closely with Tony Mowbray and Mark Venus. John added: "It's great working with these guys, they are all totally committed to our youth system.

"Tony and Mark came to us from Ipswich — one of the best clubs around at nurturing young talent — so they fully back what we are trying to do here."

John believes more of his talented young players will break into regular action with the first team in the very near future, and his top two tips are Steven Fletcher and Jamie McCluskey, both of whom were on the fringes last season.

50

### Jamie McCluskey:

Older fans would describe this tricky little player as a "tanner ba' " player with his tremendous close control and trickery.

Born in November 1987, Jamie has come through the Hibernian youth system and made his debut in season 2003/04 against Kilmarnock at Rugby Park. At just 16, he became the youngest player ever to appear in the Scottish Premier League.

Last season he went on to make a further nine league appearances under Tony Mowbray, with two more in the Scottish Cup and one in the CIS Cup – all as a substitute.

## Steven Fletcher:

It was clear from early in his development at Hibernian that Steven was something of a gem. Tall and powerful for his age, he also enjoys excellent control, pace and a keen eye for goal.

Steven, born in England in 1987, had already made five first team appearances before Tony Mowbray's arrival. However under Mogga and Mark Venus, Steven has flourished – making 26 appearances last season and scoring five goals.

He and Jamie McCluskey made a massive impact when coming on as subs in the SPL match against Dunfermline at the end of March, when Steven helped himself to a brace after the arrival of the two youngsters changed the match.

# Wearing the Armband
## – Skipper talks

Gary Caldwell was the choice of Tony Mowbray to captain the side – and such has been the leadership quality of the young international defender that the decision to give him the skipper's armband surprised no-one.

He took over from Ian Murray, promising a different approach. "Ian tends to like to lead by example. I also tend to talk a lot, to moan and cajole and try to gee up the other players. I hope I also lead by example."

"It's a great honour to be asked to captain a team like Hibernian, and I am fully aware of just how much this Club means to everyone associated with it. It's also exciting to be asked to shoulder this responsibility at a time when I believe the Club is making real progress under Tony Mowbray, Mark Venus and the rest of the management team."

"The style of football we try to play won us a lot of plaudits last season, and we will be looking to build on that. It's good that the Club strengthened in a couple of areas to increase competition for places, because competition is healthy and keeps players on their toes and performing."

"However I believe we have a good squad, with a lot of talented young players who are only going to get better as they learn more about the game through playing more games."

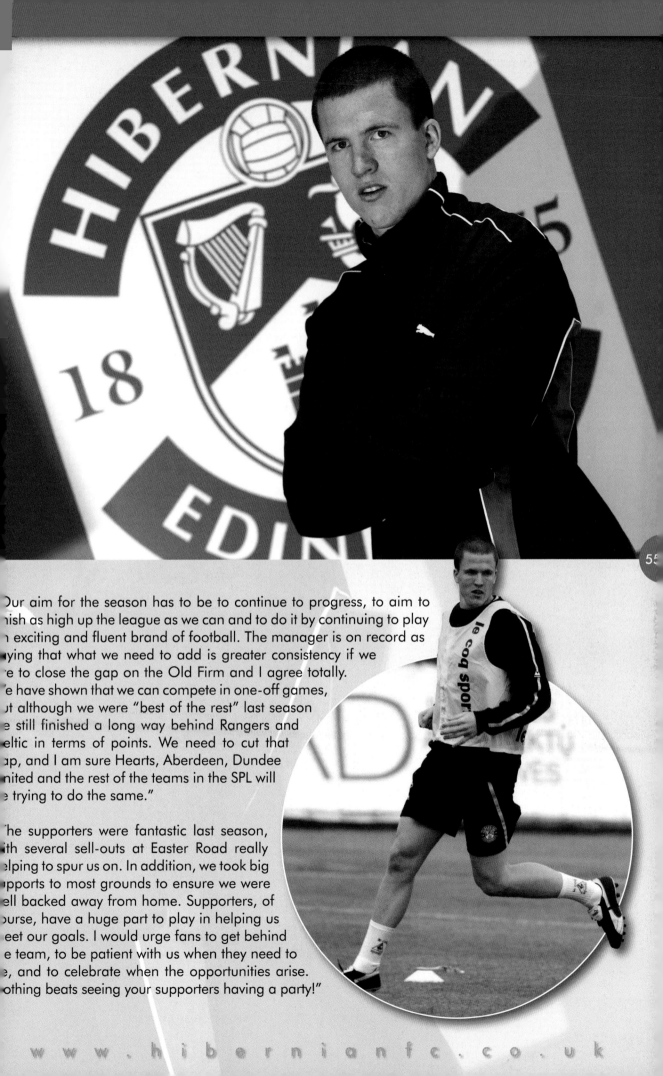

Our aim for the season has to be to continue to progress, to aim to finish as high up the league as we can and to do it by continuing to play n exciting and fluent brand of football. The manager is on record as aying that what we need to add is greater consistency if we re to close the gap on the Old Firm and I agree totally. e have shown that we can compete in one-off games, ut although we were "best of the rest" last season e still finished a long way behind Rangers and eltic in terms of points. We need to cut that ap, and I am sure Hearts, Aberdeen, Dundee nited and the rest of the teams in the SPL will e trying to do the same."

he supporters were fantastic last season, ith several sell-outs at Easter Road really elping to spur us on. In addition, we took big pports to most grounds to ensure we were ell backed away from home. Supporters, of ourse, have a huge part to play in helping us eet our goals. I would urge fans to get behind e team, to be patient with us when they need to e, and to celebrate when the opportunities arise. othing beats seeing your supporters having a party!"

# Hibernian Quiz

## Hibernian Quiz B: How well do you know your Hibernian "subjects"

### History:

1. When was the Club founded?

2. In which year did Hibernian become the first British club to play in European competition?

3. In season 1960-61 Hibernian defeated a giant of the European game in a controversial match. Which Club?

4. Who was the Manager when Hibernian played a friendly against Real Madrid in 1964?

5. Who managed the Club to League Cup success in 1972?

### Statistics:

1. Who is Hibernian's most-capped player?

2. How many times have Hibernian won the Championship?

3. Which player has made most League appearances for Hibernian, with 446?

4. The Club's record home attendance is 65,860, achieved in 1950. Against whom?

5. Who scored 364 goals for the Club – a record – during his Hibernian career?

### Geography:

1. Which South American country did the Club tour in a pioneering move in the 1950s?

2. Which Italian city club – which included legendary keeper Dino Zoff in its team – did Hibernian defeat 5-0 in 1968?

3. Where did Hibernian go on pre-season tour in July 2005?

4. Of which country was Franck Sauzee a native?

5. Which country did Joe Baker represent at full international level?

# Late Player Chat
## The new boys in town

### Michael Stewart, Midfield.
### Signed June 2005 on a one year deal.

More than a few eyebrows were raised in surprise when Tony Mowbray unveiled his first signing for the new season – midfielder Michael Stewart.

Not that the 24-year-old didn't fit the identikit of strong, skilful midfielder the gaffer had identified as a target. It was more that Michael joined Hibernian after a year-long loan spell with arch-rivals Hearts, becoming one of only a few players to cross the Capital divide.

Michael endured an injury jinxed season while on loan from Manchester United to Hearts, and found himself playing less first-team football than he would have liked. A meeting with Tony and Mark Venus convinced him that he could re-start his career at Easter Road.

At a busy Press Conference for his arrival, Michael repeatedly stressed that he had joined Hibernian in order to play football, and that he believed the passing, fluent football philosophy of the coaches would play to his strengths.

Date of Birth: 26 February 1981
Place of Birth: Edinburgh

### Zbigniew Malkowski, Goalkeeper.
### Signed July 2005 on a two year deal.

Polish goalkeeper "Zibi" was signed from Dutch aces Feyenoord, where he had spent five years being schooled without managing to break into the first team.

At 6ft 4ins tall, he is the kind of imposing goalkeeper that Tony Mowbray has been looking for to provide stiffer competition to Simon Brown for the number 1 shirt.

He made his debut on the Club's pre-season tour of Ireland, keeping clean sheets in the matches against St Patrick's and Shamrock Rovers. He said: "I was very happy to sign for Hibernian and come here to Scotland. It is a very good atmosphere with this team, a very young team and everyone wants to play for each other."

Date of Birth: 19 January 1978
Place of Birth: Olsztyn, Poland

# Derby Daze

Edinburgh Derby – the words conjured a regular mixed bag of memories for fans of either side. Losing to your biggest rival is always a sore one to take – but winning is the greatest feeling.

Everyone will have their own magic memories of this enthralling fixture, but here are a few from the record books:

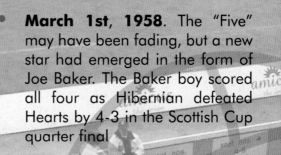

- **December 25th, 1875**, the first Edinburgh derby is played, and Hearts win 1-0.

- **April 28th, 1941** and a 16-year-old by the name of Gordon Smith makes his debut after snubbing Hearts to sign for Hibernian. The man who was to become the "Prince of Wingers" played at centre-forward that day and scored a hat-trick as Hibernian won 5-3.

- **September 20th, 1952** – an era of dominance as the "Famous Five" became the greatest forward line to grace the domestic game. Their spearhead, centre-forward Lawrie Reilly, scored a hat-trick in a 3-1 away win at Tynecastle.

- **March 1st, 1958**. The "Five" may have been fading, but a new star had emerged in the form of Joe Baker. The Baker boy scored all four as Hibernian defeated Hearts by 4-3 in the Scottish Cup quarter final

- In **January 1965** Hibernian began a period of sustained dominance with a 1-0 win. This was followed in September that year with a 4-0 win, with Hibernian scoring all four within ten minutes. Hibernian were only to lose 4 out of 32 league derbies during this era.

- **January 1st, 1973**. Hearts 0 – Hibernian 7. Hibernian greatest ever derby win, equalling Hearts worst ever league defeat. It couldn't get sweeter for Hibernian fans as a team managed by Famous Five legend Eddie Turnbull and led by the great Pat Stanton ran riot.

- **August 27th, 1994**. 62 minutes into the game Gordon Hunter scored with a close range shot to end, finally, Hearts 22-match unbeaten run in derbies.

- **19th December, 1999**. The "Millenium Derby" at Tynecastle and Hibernian run out 3-0 winners. The game ends to three empty stands, and one full of bouncing Hibernian fans.

- **October 22nd, 2000**. It gets even better as Sauzee, Latapy et al run riot and destroy Hearts by 6-2. But for some inspired goalkeeping by Anti Niema, the scoreline could have been greater. Also remembered for a Mixu Paatelainen hat-trick and spectacular display of somersaulting.

- **August 17th, 2003**. Garry O'Connor scores into injury time to grab a 1-0 home win as battling Hibernian play a big chunk of the game with 10 men following Grant Brebner's red card.

- **April 13th, 2005**. Dean Shiels pops up to smash home the winner at Tynecastle after Hibernian had ended an uninspired first-half trailing by a goal. The celebrations were very photogenic.

60

# Quiz Answers

## Quiz A: Who Said That?

1. David Murphy, on signing

2. Derek Riordan, on life

3. Gary Caldwell, signing

4. Gary O'Connor on a 40-goal partnership

5. Gary Smith, on age and experience

6. Tony Mowbray, on the last day and on qualifying

7. Guillaume Beuzelin, on his recovery

8. Antonio Murray, on international availability

9. Tony Mowbray, on Ivan Sproule

10. Jim Duffy, on Hibernian after 4-4 thriller

## Quiz B: Hibernian Subjects:

**History:**
1. 1875
2. 1955
3. Barcelona
4. Jock Stein
5. Eddie Turnbull

**Statistics:**
1. Lawrie Reilly (38 caps)
2. 4 (1902/03, 1947/48, 1950/51 and 1951/52)
3. Arthur Duncan
4. Hearts
5. Gordon Smith

**Geography:**
1. Brazil
2. Napoli
3. Ireland
4. France
5. England

# Hibs Kids

**Scotland's best Young Supporters Club has thousands of members, offers great value, includes all kinds of special offers – and best of all, it's a Hibernian club.**

Hibs Kids is open to fans under the age of 14, and costs just £10 per year. For that, Hibs Kids receive:

- Season Tickets from only £55 (over 5s) and an amazing £35 for under 5s.
- A regular Hibs Kids newsletter featuring the latest news, reviews and competitions
- Hibs Kids membership pack
- A birthday card
- Those aged 5-10 years old will be entered free into Hibernian's exclusive Mascot Draw
- 11-14 year olds will be entered free into the Hibernian Ball Person Draw
- Free access to SPL Reserve fixtures at Easter Road
- A Hibs Kids Christmas event
- Discount for Hibernian Soccer Schools for 5-12 year olds

To renew or apply for Membership simply visit the Club website at www.hibernianfc.co.uk and visit the ticket information page, or contact the Club ticket office at 12 Albion Place, Edinburgh EH7 5QG.